august 1999
Bale & Beer Bo Rass

The Gaspé Peninsula

PIERRE BEAUDOIN
and PIERRE BRUNET

From an original idea of DENIS CLERMONT
Poetry by CLAUDE LECLERC
Translation by HOWARD SCOTT

ÉDITIONS DU TRÉCARRÉ

Graphic artists
Martine Maksud
André Pettigrew

Typesetting
Ateliers de typographie Collette Inc.

ISBN 2-89249-319-6 (soft bound)
ISBN 2-89249-322-6 (hard bound)

Legal deposit
Bibliothèque nationale du Québec

Printed in Canada

Éditions du Trécarré
Saint-Laurent (Québec) Canada

1 2 3 4 5   94 93 92 91 90

Voyagers to the Gaspé,
tarry a while, for you will never
be able to go farther...

You have arrived
at the beginning of time.

CONTENTS

...sky and sea

Cap Blanc and Bonaventure Island

A bird flies over a silvery sea, carrying along the riches of an ephemeral world.

Barachois, Percé

Grasses grow out of that strange place where land and sea merge.

Cove at Beaufils

The stormy sea breaks over age-old rocks that crumble at the slow pace of imaginary seasons.

Statues by M. Gagnon, Sainte-Flavie

A row of statues bear silent witness to humanity's will to survive its destiny.

Percé Rock

Alone, this rock stands like a giant boat split asunder by the fury of time.

Baie-des-Sables

Red rocks streaked with grey swell up through a stony beach.

Bonaventure Island, Percé

What are these great white birds? Gannets come to haunt our shores.

Percé Rock

An ancient rock flooded with sunlight stands guard over a sleeping sea.

Pic de l'Aurore (Dawn Peak)

Steadfast evergreens cling to the flanks of a giant peak.

Mont Saint-Pierre

A storm-weary sea comes to rest on quiet shores.

Mont Saint-Pierre

A little house from times gone by proudly endures through the cycle of the seasons.

Gaspé Provincial Park

18

In a lost land, a lake so blue that all who see it fall in love.

Sainte-Anne-des-Monts

At dawn, everything melts into a world of dreams. Reality returns only with the coming of day.

20

Waves of fog-blanketed mountains flow lazily under a complacent sky.

Cap Blanc, Percé

The waters of the night brush an indifferent shore in a laconic to and fro.

Percé

22

The moon occupies the fragile space between sky and sea.

Gaspé

23

Under the kindly sky, a shady mountain watches over a meadow tinged with pink, and slowly loses its gloom.

...earth and rock

Percé

26

To an indifferent rock, flowers sing a springtime melody that stirs only the wind.

Percé Rock

Percé Rock

After centuries of battle,
the sea has breached the walls of the weary rock.

This rock with its shattered walls :
does it secretly fear the tempestuous sea ?

27

Bonaventure Island

Thousands of birds return each year to sing in unison the joy of gathering.

Percé Rock

A rock held prisoner by a tyrannical sea secretly dreams of being free once again.

Gaspé region

Verdant landscapes mysteriously preserve the purity of change.

Pic de l'Aurore, Percé

The sea stirs at dawn, its waves nervously touching the foot of the sleeping cliff.

View of Percé from Cap-Barré

Isolated land on steep shores where a timeless, ageless village is hidden.

Gaspé

A rainbow, born between the earth and the sea, colors as it passes all the hopes of eternity.

View from Pic de l'Aurore

Proud cape that has faced the sea for thousands of years, never yielding.

Bonaventure Island

This meadow of wild grasses and scented flowers would be so wonderful to roll in before the summer ends.

Les Méchins

36

The waves of the bay, deepest blue, brush the misty curves of a deserted beach.

Mont Albert

Autumn has barely begun when the yellowed leaves, trembling, tell us of the great frosts to come.

Forillon Park

38

Laughing waters, dancing waters invite nature to a huge celebration.

Mont Jacques-Cartier

You are king of our forests, a symbol of strength and perseverance, like our pioneers who built new worlds.

Gaspé Provincial Park

River, will you tell me one day the wondrous secret of your singing waters?

Mont Albert

Huge forests stretching to infinity, what are the secrets of your mottled landscape?

Gaspé region

Pretty daisies, that die all too soon, will you come back next spring to intoxicate the meadows?

Murdochville region

All year long, the elegant aspens dress up the forest with their ever-changing finery.

Forillon Park

Trees burst in life with a million leaves and the forest becomes a dazzling mirage.

Métis-sur-Mer

45

Wild flowers that have chosen the freedom of the meadows.

Gannets, Bonaventure Island

46

Tender the touch of a loving beak...

Barachois

A century-old house silently tells the history of the land.

...steeple and spire

Bonaventure Island

A weathered chapel carries the weight of years.

The flowery field brightens the old walls and we forget for a moment the fading of age.

Saint-Georges-de-Malbaie

Bright white church that rang with the prayers of those who went down to the sea.

Sainte-Marthe-de-Gaspé Parish

The mid-day sun shines through golden stained glass onto the polished floor of a beautiful little church.

Jacques Cartier monument, Gaspé

A worthy monument to the valiant efforts of a fearless explorer.

Mont Albert

Immemorial liquid joy and the endless laughter of the Earth.

Percé

Old steeple from which the bells once rang out, now you silently slumber in the shadow of the forest.

Headland on the Madeleine River

Red-roofed, white-walled houses keep their old secrets from passersby.

Saint-Majorique, Gaspé

A man has chosen for his final resting-place a land that is friend to sky and to water.

Saint-Maurice-de-l'Échouerie

Under the warmth of the sun's rays, a whole village languidly surrenders to summer.

Rivière-au-Renard

My village lives twixt the land and sea, and everything here is so pure and beautiful that it seems like paradise.

Mont Albert

Purest white and colors of dreams. Signs of the serenity of this deep emerald country.

Percé

The cross of the day invites passersby to pause and contemplate.

Percé

The cross of the night watches over the sleeping villagers.

Belle-Anse, Percé

A grey-clad house silently watches over its friend, the sea.

Percé

Houses glowing with friendly warmth welcome us to this green valley.

Causapscal, Matapédia Valley

An icy river slowly winds through a tender bed of snow.

Mont Albert Inn

The rising fog slowly reveals the quiet beauty of a lonely inn.

Gaspé train station

From village to village, you follow your route through an ageless landscape, and return to your source.

Percé

Sad little station abandoned by the trains that no longer take the time to stop.

Percé

I dream of leaving for far-off lands. Little train, will you take me away?

Percé

These benches look lonely. Where are the travellers who will come to warm them?

Mont Albert Inn

A tiny building delights visitors with its happy mix of white and grey.

Barachois

73

Life sleeps through the fourth season. In the spring, it will wake again.

Amqui

74

Broad fields of snow surround my house, gripping it in the long chill of winter.

Barachois

White, all white. Even the little church has donned its frosty cloak.

Routhierville, Matapédia

Could this bridge tell us the gentle secrets of the people of bygone days ?

Matapédia

Winter is always undressing before the curious eyes of a village.

...rigging and tide

Causapscal

The hamlet lies peaceful and contented in the valley. Will the insistent rays of the sun rouse it ?

Cap-des-Rosiers

Percé

What does this lighthouse see far off on the horizon?
It seems like a witness to a dying world.

Tell me, old accordion-player,
why is your music so sad?

La Martre

Sleepy lighthouse, red and white, don't you see the sailors coming in the distance?

Saint-Georges-de-Malbaie

Drying cod, a silent reminder of long days of fishing.

84

These stacked pots will soon become, beneath the sea, false refuges for bewitched lobsters.

Barachois

At nightfall, an abandoned boat secretly dreams of living again in the morning.

Percé

Fishermen share their work, and perhaps a few playful secrets.

View of Percé from Mont Sainte-Anne

A magic corner of land rubs shoulders with the sea in happy union.

Percé

A beautiful bird says to the child, " Climb on my wings and I'll show you a continent."

Gros Morne

A green boat, a red boat — are they bored on this wide grey beach?

90

Land-locked boat. Will you soon be floating on the waves again?

Saint-Georges-de-Malbaie

This fishing dock will soon come alive as the boats take to the sea.

Madeleine

An eery moment as day breaks after an all-too-brief dawn.

Matane

A boat's lights and their strange reflections execute a forbidden dance.

94

Imprisoned boats patiently await the next tide.

The Madeleine River

A happy harmony of form and color.

Special thanks to our sponsors without whom this book would still be a dream.

William Boulay of
ALPHONSE OUELLETTE's Garage
in collaboration with
BUDGET car leasing

Richard Jarry of KODAK

Guy Authier and Réal Payette of
NIKON CANADA INC.

The visitors of the Gaspé peninsula will find at the tourist halt Menoumm, in Tourelle, a wide range of fresh seafood products and quality souvenirs.

Charles Leprohon,
director of customer service,
and Gérald Girouard,
director of operations at
AUTOMOBILES NISSAN DU CANADA LTÉE.

Daniel Rosseel,
director of public relations,
and Marcel Bordeleau,
assistant-director at
VIA RAIL CANADA INC.

Jean-Louis Couture
of Le Gîte du
Mont Albert

Michel Faugère of
PUBLIPHOTO

Jacques Beaudin of
L.R. VIALA INC.

VALAN PHOTOS

Colour separation:
P.R. LITHO

96

PIERRE BEAUDOIN

Pierre Beaudoin did his studies in graphic design and commercial photography.
He is currently a member of the Professional Photographers of Québec, and his photos appear regularly in a number of magazines. He has also worked as a free-lancer for the Québec Ministry of Tourism and on commercial projects. For the last few years, he has devoted himself to photojournalism, in the broad sense of the word.
In 1987, he collaborated with Pierre Brunet on the book "Charlevoix."

Cover

pages

7   9   10   11   12   13   14   16   17   18   20   21
22   27   28   31   34   35   36   37   40   45   46   50
54   55   68   69   70   71   73   81   82   83   84   85
86   87   88   89   90   91   92   93   94

PIERRE BRUNET

Trained in graphic design, Pierre Brunet gradually developed an interest in photography and, since the beginning of the 70s, he has moved more and more into landscape and nature work for which he has a particular fondness. His work has appeared in many magazines and tourist brochures, including publications of the Québec Ministry of Tourism, and in several series of diaries and calendars. In 1987, he collaborated with Pierre Beaudoin on the book "Charlevoix," a collection of 104 photographs. He specializes in seascapes and landscapes of Canada and Europe.

pages

8   15   19   23   26   29   30   32   33   38   41   42
43   44   47   51   52   53   56   57   58   59   60   61
62   63   64   65   66   67   72   74   75   76   77   80
95

MICHEL BOURQUE   page 39